ONCE YOU COMMI
MIND THAT YOU I
YOU WANT, IT
IMPLEMENT TO B

G000291572

THE MASTER KEY TO WEALTH

DR. JOSEPH MURPHY

THE MASTER KEY TO WEALTH

The whole world and all its treasures, in the sea, air and earth, were here when you were born. Begin to think of the untold and undiscovered riches all around you, waiting for the intelligence of man to bring them forth. Look at wealth as the air you breath; get that attitude of mind. As Emerson said to the woman - you know, who wanted to prosper - he took her down to the ocean, he said, "Take a look". She said, "Oh, there's plenty of water, isn't there?" He said, "Look at wealth that way, and you'll always have it." Yes, realize it's like the tide, forever flowing out, forever flowing back.

A sales manager said to me that an associate of his sold a million dollar idea for expansion to the organization. You can have an idea worth a fortune, too. Wealth is a thought-image in your mind. Wealth is an idea in your mind. Wealth is a mental attitude. He also told me that there were more millionaires now in the United States than at any time in the history of the country. You can have an idea worth a fortune - yes, you can. Moreover, you are here to release the imprisoned spender within you and surround yourself with luxury, beauty and the riches of life.

I learned that it is necessary to have the right attitude towards money, wealth, food, raiment, clothing - all these things. When you really make friends with wealth, you will always have a surplus of it. It is normal and natural for you to desire a fuller, richer, happier and more wonderful life. Look upon money as God's idea of maintaining the economic health of the nation, of the nations of the world.

When money is circulating freely in your life, you're economically healthy, in the same manner as when your blood is circulating freely, you're free from congestion. Begin now to see money in its true significance and role in life as a symbol of exchange - that's all it is. It has taken many forms down through the ages. Money to you should mean freedom from want. It should mean beauty, luxury, abundance, sense of security and refinement. You're entitled to it.

Being poor is a disease. It is a mental attitude. A young woman, a very good writer who had had several articles accepted for publication, said to me one time, "I don't write for money". I said to her, "What's wrong with money? It's true you don't write for money, but the labor is worthy of its hire. What you write inspires, lifts up and encourages others. When you adopt the right attitude, financial compensation will automatically come to you, freely and copiously.

She actually disliked money; you know, once she referred to money as "filthy luker", going back, I suppose, to those early days where she heard mother or somebody say "money is evil", you know, or "love of money is the root of all evil", and all these things, without any understanding at all. It's a rank superstition to say money is "evil" or "filthy luker". This woman had a subconscious pattern that there was some virtue in poverty. There isn't! It's a sickness, a disease. I explained to her that there was no evil in the universe, and that good and evil were in the thoughts and motivations of man. All evil comes from misinterpretations of life and misuse of the laws of mind. In other words, the only evil is ignorance, and the only consequence is suffering.

It would be foolish to pronounce uranium, silver, lead, copper, iron, cobalt, nickel, calcium, or a dollar bill "evil". How absurd, grotesque, and stupid that is! The only difference between one metal and another is the number and rate of motions of electrons revolving around a central nucleus. A piece of paper, such as a hundred dollar bill, is innocuous, and the only difference between it and a copper or lead is that the atoms and molecules with their electrons and protons are arranged differently for the physical evidences of money.

Here is a simple technique she practiced which multiplied wealth in her experience:

"My writings go forth to bless, heal, inspire, elevate and dignify the minds and hearts of men and women. And I am divinely compensated in a wonderful way. I look upon money as divine substance, where everything is made from the One Spirit. I know matter and spirit are one. Money is constantly circulating in my life and I use it wisely and constructively. Money flows to me freely, joyously and endlessly. Money is an idea in the mind of God; it is good and very good."

That's a wonderful prayer. It eradicates that superstitious nonsense about money being evil and things of that nature, or "there's some virtue in poverty", or "the Lord loves the poor". All of that is rank superstition. It is frightful ignorance, that's all it is.

This young lady's changed attitude towards money has worked wonders in her life. It'll work wonders in your life, too. And she has completely eradicated that strange, superstitious belief that money was "filthy luker". She realized that her silent condemnation of money caused money to fly from her, instead of to her. Her income has tripled in three months, which was just the beginning of her financial prosperity.

Some years ago I talked with a clergyman who had a very good following. He had an excellent knowledge of the laws of mind, and was able to impart this knowledge to others. But he could never make ends meet.

Love in Biblical language is to give your allegiance, loyalty and faith to the source of all things, which is God, or the Living Spirit, or the Life Principal in you. You are not, therefore, to give your allegiance, loyalty and trust to created things, but to the creator, the eternal source of everything in the universe, the source of your own breath, the source of your life, the source of the hair on your head, the source of your heartbeat, the source of the sun and the moon and the stars, the source of the world.

If a man says, "All I want is money, nothing else; that's my God and nothing but money matters", he can get it, of course. But he is here to lead a balanced life. Man must also claim peace, harmony, beauty, guidance, love, joy, wholeness, in all phases of his life. How can he live without courage, faith, love, good will, joy in this world today? Nothing wrong with money - not a thing in the world, but that's not the sole aim in life. To make money the sole aim in life would constitute an error, a wrong choice. There wouldn't be anything evil in it, but you'd be imbalanced and lopsided. You must express you hidden talents; you must find your true place in life; you must experience the joy of contributing to the growth, happiness and success of others. We're all here to give, and give of your talents to the world. God gave you everything; God gave you himself. You have a tremendous debt to pay because you owe everything you have to the infinite. Therefore you're here to give life and love and truth to your ideals, to your dreams, your aspirations; you're here to row the boat, put your hands at the wheel, contribute to the success and happiness not only of your children, but of the whole world.

To accumulate money to the exclusion of everything else causes man to become imbalanced and lopsided, and frustrated. Yes, as you apply the laws of your subconscious in the right way, you can have all the money you want, and still have peace of mind, harmony, wholeness and serenity. You can do a lot of good with it. You can use it wisely, judiciously and constructively, like anything in nature. You can use your knowledge or philosophy in a constructive way, or you can begin to brainwash impressionable minds with communism and all the rest of it.

I pointed out to this minister how he was completely misinterpreting the Scripture in pronouncing pieces of paper or metals "evil", when these were neutral substances where there is nothing good or bad but thinking makes it so. He began to see all the good he could do with more money for his wife, family and parishioners. He changed his attitude and let go of the superstition. He began to claim boldly, regularly and systematically: "Infinite spirit reveals better ways for me to serve. I am inspired and illumined from on high, and I give a divine transfusion of faith and confidence in the one presence and power to all those who hear me. I look upon money as God's idea, and it is constantly circulating in my life and that of all the people who surround me. We use it wisely, judiciously and constructively under God's guidance and God's wisdom".

This young clergyman made a habit of this prayer, knowing that it would activate the powers of his subconscious mind. Today he has a beautiful church which he wanted; the people built it for him. He has a radio program and has all the money he needs for his personal, worldly and cultural needs. I can assure you he no longer criticizes money; if you do, it'll fly away from you, because you're condemning that which you're praying for.

Now follow this technique which I'm going to outline for you, and you'll never want for wealth all the days of your life, for it is the Master Key to wealth.

The first step is to reason it out in your mind that God or the Life Principal, or the Living Spirit is the source of the universe, the galaxies in space, and everything you see, whether you look at the stars in the sky, the mountains, the lakes, the deposits in the earth and the sea, or all animals and plants. The Life Principal gave birth to you and all the powers, qualities and attributes of God are within you. Come to a simple conclusion, that everything you see and are aware of, came out of the invisible mind of the infinite, or the Life Principal; and that everything that man has invented, created or made, came out of the invisible mind of man; and the mind of man and the mind of God are one, for there's only one mind. That mind is common to all individual men. Everyone is an inlet and outlet to all that is.

Come now to a clear-cut decision that God is the source of your supply of energy, vitality, health, creative ideas; the source of the sun, the air you breathe, the apple you eat, and the money in your pocket. For everything is made inside and out of the invisible. It is as easy for God to become wealth in your life, as it is to become a blade of grass or a crystal of snow.

The second step: Decide now to engrave in your subconscious mind the idea of wealth; ideas that convey to the subconscious, by repetition, faith and expectancy. By repeating a thought pattern or an act over and over again, it becomes automatic, and your subconscious - being compulsive - you will be compelled to express wealth. The pattern is the same as learning to walk, swim, play the piano, type, or drive a car. You must believe in what you're affirming; it's not mumbo-jumbo; it's not idle affirmations. You must believe in what you're affirming like you believe that when you put seeds in the ground they grow after their kind. And the seeds are thoughts, deposited in your own subconscious mind. Realize that what you are affirming is like the apple seeds you deposit in the ground and they grow after their kind. You could imagine the seeds going from your conscious to your subconscious mind and being reproduced on the screen of space.

By watering and fertilizing these seeds you accelerate their growth. Know what you are doing and why you are doing it. You're writing it with your conscious pen in your subconscious mind, because you know wealth is - walk down the street and you see it. Can you count the flowers along the road as you drive; can you count the sands in the seashore; can you count the stars in the sky; can you count the wealth that you're walking on? Yes, underneath you, may be oil, gold, silver, uranium. Do you ever think of the riches of the sea, the soil, the air?

The third step is, repeat the following affirmation for about five minutes, night and morning: "I am now writing in my subconscious mind the idea of God's wealth. God is the source of my supply, and I know God is the Life Principal within me, and I know I'm alive. And all my needs are met at every moment of time and point of space. God's wealth flows freely, joyously and ceaselessly into my experience and I give thanks for God's riches forever circulating in my experience."

Step Four: When thoughts of lack come to you, such as "I can't afford that trip", or "I can't meet that note in the bank", or "I can't pay that bill", never, never finish a negative statement about finances. This is mandatory. Reverse it immediately in your mind by affirming: "God is my instant and everlasting supply, and that bill is paid in divine order". If a negative thought comes to you fifty times in one hour, reverse it each time by thinking and affirming: "God is my instant supply, meeting that need right now." After a while, the thought of financial lack will lose all momentum and you will find your subconscious is being conditioned to wealth.

If you look at a new car, for example, never say: "I can't buy that", or "I can't afford it." Your subconscious takes you literally and blocks all your good. On the contrary, say to yourself, "That car is for sale; it is a divine idea and I accept it in divine order through divine love". This is the Master Key to wealth! It's impossible for any sincere person to practice this technique and not have all the wealth he or she needs all the days of your life.

So follow it, and you're setting the law of opulence in operation. It will work for you as well as for anybody else. The law of mind is no respecter of persons. Your thoughts make you wealthy or poor. Choose the riches of life, right here and right now.

A sales manager sent me one of his men for counseling. This salesman was a brilliant, college graduate; he knew his products very well. He was in a lucrative territory, but was making only $5,000 annually in commissions. The sales manager felt he should double or at least triple it. In talking to the young man, I found he was down on himself. He had developed a subconscious pattern or self-image of $5000 a year; in other words, "that's all I'm worth". He said that he had been born in a poverty-stricken home and that his parents had told him that he was destined to be poor. His stepfather had always told him, "You'll never amount to anything"; "You're dumb"; "You're stupid". These thoughts were accepted by his impressionable mind, and he was experiencing his subconscious belief in lack and limitation.

I explained to him that he could change his subconscious mind by feeding it with life-giving patterns. Accordingly, I gave him a mental and spiritual formula to follow which would transform his life. I explained to him that he should under no circumstances deny what he had affirmed because his subconscious mind accepted what he really believed.

Your subconscious mind accepts your convictions -- what you really believe. So believe in God's wealth and God's riches, which are all around you, by the way.

He affirmed every morning before going to work: "I am born to succeed. I am born to win. The infinite within me can't fail. Divine law and order govern my life. Divine peace fills my soul. Divine love saturates my mind. Infinite intelligence guides me in all ways. God's riches flow to me freely, joyously, endlessly, ceaselessly. I am advancing, moving forward and growing, mentally, spiritually, financially and in all other ways. I know these truths are sinking into my subconscious mind, and I know and I believe they will row after their kind."

A year later when I met this young man again, I discovered that he had been transformed. He had absorbed these ideas which we had discussed, and he said: "I am appreciating life now, and wonderful things have happened. I have an income of $25,000 this year, five times greater than the previous year". He has learned the simple truth that whatever he inscribes in his subconscious mind becomes affective and functional in his life. That power is within you. You can use it also.

The young boy who's operating this machine while I am broadcasting, his name is Robbie Wright, and he told me about his uncle who used to work in a bank. And this uncle wanted to make more money for his wife and his children, and he was always affirming, you know: "God is my instant supply; I am divinely guided in all ways; infinite spirit opens up a new door". Well, he told me that his uncle was in town about two months ago and that his salary now was $200,000 a year, all his expenses paid, and he was getting $40,000 when he started to realize the truth about himself, and he's able to do great things, and living a wonderful life down south in another state.

All of this is an idea; all it was was an idea in his mind. Wealth is an idea. A radio is an idea. Television is an idea. An automobile is an idea. Everything you look at is an idea! Suppose you destroyed all the automobiles in the world due to some holocaust. Well, an engineer could run them off, couldn't he? And we'd have millions of them in no time!

Use the following meditation for assurance in achieving financial wealth: "Thou madest him to have dominion over the works of thy hands. I know that my faith in God determines my future. My faith in God means my faith in all things good. I unite myself now with true ideas, and I know the future will be the image and likeness of my habitual thinking. As a man thinketh in his heart or subconscious, so is he. From this moment forward, my thoughts are on whatsoever things are true, whatsoever things are honest, whatsoever things are just, whatsoever things are lovely and of good report. Day and night I meditate on these things, and I know these seeds, which are thoughts, which I habitually dwell upon, will become a rich harvest for me. I am the captain of my soul; I am the master of my fate, for my thought and feeling are my destiny".

You see prayers and affirmations are not for the purpose of changing God or the Living Spirit, or the Life Principal, or influencing the divine. God is the same yesterday, today and forever. You don't change God, but you align yourself mentally with that which was always true. You don't create harmony; harmony is. You don't create love; God is love and that love of God is within you. You don't create peace; God is peace and God indwells you. But you must claim that the peace of God floods your mind. You must claim that the harmony of God is in your home, in your pocketbook, in your business, and in all phases of your life.

All of good is available to each of us. Our prayers and affirmations are for the purpose of bringing our own mind to the point where we can accept the gifts which were given to us from the foundation of time. And God is the giver and the gift. The oil was in the ground before you were born, before any man walked the earth; so was gold and silver, uranium and lead, copper and all the metals that we use today. They were all there. Didn't it take a little intelligence from the mind of man to find these things? Yes. So, if you send two men to Utah and one man is a geologist, or he may be also a mineralogist, and he finds nothing; another man goes and in the first five minutes he finds a vein of uranium or silver in the same territory, in the same land. Where was the wealth? The wealth was in the mind of the second man. He believed in a guiding principal. The other fellow found nothing. He was walking on it.

So there is a guiding principal that will lead you. That's what led men to find gold and silver and oil and lead and all these things. We don't need to work on conditions; we need only to work on ourselves. The only place we can cure our lack and limitation is in our own mind being transformed by the law of your mind. When we have done it, there we shall find that the world - that is, your body, your environment and conditions - will be a mathematical reflection of your inner state of mind. "Whatsoever things he ask for when he pray, believe that he hath received them and he shall have them". That is the basis of all successful prayer, whether for the healing of our bodies or prosperities, success, for achievement, or for material benefits. Once you convince your deeper mind that you have the thing you want, it will proceed immediately to bring it to pass.

You might say to me, "How can I convince my deeper mind, my subconscious, that I have riches or any other good thing when my common sense tells me that bills are piling up, creditors are after me, the bank is calling up to pay for the mortgage for the money I owe?" and so on. You can't. If you keep thinking about debts and obligations and how much you owe, you'll only magnify your misery. But here is the truth about the laws of your mind. Your deeper mind accepts as a fact whatever you repeat to it in convincing tones often enough, just the same as you learned to walk. You had a thought pattern, an act - whether it was swimming or walking or playing tennis or golf - and you repeat it over and over again; you knew what you were doing and why you were doing it. You want to learn to walk, you want to learn to dance, you want to learn to swim. So finally your subconscious assimilated the pattern, didn't it? And then you swim automatically and you walk automatically.

The same procedure in praying for wealth or anything else. Once your subconscious accepts the statement as a fact, it proceeds to do everything possible to bring riches to you. Now that's the whole purpose of affirmations: so that you convince yourself of the truth of that which you affirm. Then your deeper mind will bring these things to pass.

Many men say to me, "Oh, I got an affirmation from someone, and it said I am rich and prosperous now, I am successful and I'm very wealthy. That affirmation succeeded in making me much more aware of my need". Because you see, he believed more in poverty and lack than he did in the riches all around him. So I explained to him, I said, "You must turn away from that pattern and come back, change your belief. Your subconscious accepts what you believe. I said, "Look around you, and realize that God created you and the whole world. It's an invisible spirit within you. Everything is made inside and out of it. It started your heartbeat. It's the air you breathe, the water you drink; it's the fruit that you eat. Therefore turn away and turn within, and change that and say, "I recognize the eternal source of my supply. God is the source of my supply. All my needs - spiritual, mental, material - are met at every moment of time and point of space. And God's wealth is circulating in my life and there is always a surplus, so by day and by night I'm advancing, moving forward and growing, spiritually, mentally, materially, financially, intellectually - in every way. And all things be ready if the mind be so. It is done unto me as I believe, and before they call I will answer, while they're yet speaking I will hear. Oh, how I love thy law. Let it be my meditation both day and night. And the law is I am what I contemplate. I am what I believe myself to be. According to my faith is it done unto me."

God gave you richly all things to enjoy. God made you rich; why then are you poor? And as he began to realize the source of the infinite ocean supply, the source of the very hair on his head, you know, the source of the power that enables him to lift up a chair, the source of the grass, the source of the hay in the field, the source of the cattle, he began to realize the source and he aligned himself with it. And then it made sense to him, and then he realized that he was writing in his subconscious mind the idea of wealth, of growth, and prosperity.

He changed his belief to a belief in the riches, the endless riches all around him, instead of poverty which was a false belief in his mind. Don't you know there's enough fruit in the tropics to feed all humanity? Nature is lavish, extravagant, and bountiful.

God gave you, richly, yes, all things to enjoy.

These things he said, "I've set unto you that my joy might remain in you and your joy might be full. Heretofore you'll ask for nothing; now ask that your joy might be full. And I am come that you might have life, and have it more abundantly. Heretofore, you've asked for nothing; now ask, that your joy might be full." But to ask, you see, in the Bible is to CLAIM.

So, if you have a lot of debts and obligations, a lot of bills to pay - don't worry about them. Turn to the source which is endless. Remember the farmer, what he says to you. He says, "Well, I don't worry about the weeds. The grain is growing and it will kill all the weeds". That's what the farmer tells you. Likewise, are you focused on your good, on guidance and right action, on the eternal source of your supply, whether it is mental or spiritual or financial you need? It is but one source, not two. And as you turn to it and give thanks for that endless supply, then all the weeds will be killed. Thoughts of lack and limitation will die in you, and God will multiply your good exceedingly.

To bring joy into your life, pray for joy by claiming it. "The joy of the Lord is my strength", the Bible says. Repeat that to yourself and after a while, you'll be amazed what will happen to your blood stream and to the general circulation. Don't keep analyzing it or gritting your teeth about it; just know that joy is the expression of life.   Don't work like a horse at it; use no will power, no muscle power. No blood vessel power is involved in this mental and spiritual therapeutic technique. Just know and claim that the joy of the Lord is flowing through you now and wonders will happen as you pray this way. Freedom and peace of mind will be yours as a result. If you have peace of mind, you'll have peace in your pocketbook, in your home, in your relationship with people, for peace is the power, the heart of God. The city of God is your mind and the people who dwell there, for you know very well who dwells there: your thoughts, ideas, images, beliefs, opinions. Make sure they conform to the divine standard.

A woman said to me, "I was blocked financially. I had reached the point where I had not enough money for food for the children. All I had was five dollars. I held it in my hand and said, 'God will multiply this exceedingly, according to his riches and glory. I am now filled with the riches of the infinite. All my needs are instantaneously met now and all the days of my life."

Now she believed that; it wasn't idle words. You don't gain the ear of God by vain repetitions. No, you must know what you're doing and why you're doing it. You must know that your conscious mind is a pen and you're writing something, engraving something in your subconscious mind. And whatever you impress your subconscious mind with, will be expressed on the screen of space. It will come forth as form, function, experience and events - good or bad. So make sure you plant that which is lovely and of good report.

She said, "I affirmed that 'All my needs are instantaneously met now and all the days of my life', for about a half an hour, and a great sense of peace came over me. I spent the five dollars freely for food. The owner of the market asked me if I wanted to work there as a cashier, since the present one had just gotten married and left. I accepted it, and shortly afterwards I married the owner - my boss - and we have experienced, and are experiencing, all the riches of life.

This woman looked to the source. She didn't know how her prayer would be answered, because you never know the workings of the subconscious. She believed in her heart in the blessings of the infinite. Follow: To believe is to live in the state of being it. It also means to be alive to the eternal truths. Her good was magnified and multiplied exceedingly because the subconscious always magnifies what you give attention to.

There is a presence and a power within you and you can use it, and you can stir up the gift of God within you, for God is the giver and the gift, and everything has been given to you. And therefore you can tune in and claim guidance, right action, beauty, love, peace, abundance, security. You can say to yourself, "Well, God's ideas unfold within me, bringing me harmony, health, peace and joy" - during business, you're a professional man. You're an artist, an inventor - just sit down quietly and say, "God reveals to me new, creative ideas; original, wonderful ideas which bless humanity in countless ways." And then watch the wonderful ideas come to you. And they will come, because when you call, it answers. Remember what is says in the Bible? "Call upon me, I'll answer you; I'll be with you in trouble; I set you on high because you will know my name". And the name means the nature. Well, the nature of infinite intelligence is responsiveness. Call, the response comes.

Constantly affirm, feel and believe that God multiplies your good exceedingly and you will be enriched every moment of the day spiritually, mentally, intellectually, financially and socially, for there is no end to the glory of man for his daily living. Watch the wonders that will happen as you impress these truths in your subconscious mind.

As you read this book, let these truths seep into your subconscious, and they will, and they are, and you're engraving them. The more often you do this, well the quicker you will impregnate your deeper mind. You'll experience a glorious future in a financial way; in every way, too.

Watch your thoughts. Never talk about economic lack and limitation. Never talk about being poor, or in want. It is very foolish to talk to your neighbors or relatives about hard times, financial problems, and like matters. Count your blessings. Begin to think prosperous thoughts. Talk about the divine riches present everywhere. Realize that the feeling of wealth produces wealth.

When you talk about not having enough to go around, and how little you have, and how you must cut corners and eat the cheapest meat, these thoughts are created. And you are only impoverishing yourself. Use the money, you know, freely. Release it with joy and realize that God's wealth flows to you in avalanches of abundance. Look up to the source. As you turn to the divine presence within you, the response will come.

It is written, "He careth for you".

You will find neighbors, strangers, and associates, adding to your good and also to your supply of material things. Make it a practice to pray for divine guidance in all your ways, and believe that God or the supreme intelligence is supplying all your needs according to his riches and glory.

Claim it boldly. And grace, when it's removed from its mystique, is simply the mathematical, orderly reflection of you habitual thinking and imagery. In other words, there's supreme intelligence that responds to your conscious thinking and imagery.

Pray for divine guidance, therefore, in all your ways. As you make a habit of this attitude of mind, you will find the invisible law of opulence can and will produce visible riches for you.

Recently a doctor told me that her constant prayer was as follows: "I live in the joyous expectancy of the best, and invariably the best comes to me. My favorite Bible verse with which I saturate my mind is: 'He giveth to all life and breath and all things".

She has learned that she is not dependent on people for joy, health, success, and happiness or peace of mind. She looks to the Living Spirit Almighty within her, for promotion, achievement, wealth, success and happiness. "Whosoever trusteth in the Lord, happy is he". That's from the book of Proverbs, sixteenth chapter, twentieth verse. Contemplate promotion, success, achievement, illumination, and inspiration, and the spirit of the Almighty will move on your behalf, compelling you to express fully what you meditate on. Let go know and permit the infinite riches of the infinite one to open up new doors for you, and let wonders happen in your life.

In prayer therapy, avoid struggle and strain. Don't try and force things; how could you add power to omnipotence? Can you make a seed grow? You can't. Plant it in the ground; it will grow. The oak is in the acorn; the apple is in the apple seed. The archetype or pattern is there, but you must deposit it in the soil, where it dies - undergoes dissolution to squeeze its energy into another form of itself.

Spiritual-minded man, he looks at an acorn and he sees a forest. Yes, that's the way your subconscious works: it magnifies your good exceedingly. So avoid strain, since this attitude is indicative of your own belief. If you're worried, and fearful and anxious, well, that inhibits your good. That brings about blocks and delays and impediments in your life. What does fear do? "That which I greatly fear has come upon me". Reverse this: "That which I greatly love comes into my experience". Love is an emotional attachment.

In your subconscious is all the wisdom and power necessary to solve any problem. Your conscious mind is prone to look at external conditions and tends continually to struggle and to resist. Remember, however, it is the quiet mind that gets things done.

Quiet your body periodically. Tell it to be still and relax; it has to obey you. Your body moves as moved upon. Your body acts as acted upon. Your body has no self-conscious intelligence, no volition, no will. It moves as moved upon. You can play a melody of God on your body. When your conscious mind is quiet and receptive, the wisdom of your subconscious rises to the surface mind and you receive your solution.

A beauty parlor operator told me that the secret of her success was that every morning, prior to opening her beauty salon, she had a quiet period in which she affirms: "God's peace fills my soul, and God's love saturates my whole being. God guides, prospers and inspires me. I am illumined from on high, and his healing love flows from me to all my clients. Divine love comes in my door; divine love goes out of my door. All those who come into my salon are blessed, healed, and inspired. The infinite healing presence saturates the whole place. This is the day the Lord hath made, and I rejoice and give thanks for the countless blessings which come to my clients and to myself".

She had this prayer written out on a card, and reiterates these truths every morning. At night she gives thanks for all her clients, claiming that they're guided, prospered, happy and harmonious, and that God and his love flow through each one, filling up all the empty vessels in her life. She stated to me that following this prayer technique pattern, at the end of three months she had far more clients than she could handle and had to hire three additional operators. She had discovered the riches of effective prayer and is prospering beyond her fondest dreams.

A sales manager told me that he had been fired because of excessive drinking on the job, and because of being involved with one of the secretaries in the office. He was very distressed, dejected and worried about his wife, his income, and his future. In talking with his wife later, I discovered that she was a chronic nagger and had tried unsuccessfully to dominate and control her husband. She was abnormally jealous and very possessive, and she clocked him in every evening, creating a scene if he were not home at a certain hour.

He was emotionally and spiritually immature, and did not handle the matter at all constructively. He deeply resented her nagging and her clocking of his arrival at home, and retaliated by drinking and becoming involved with another woman. He said to me, "I just wanted to get even with her". Both of them agreed it takes two, you know, to make a go of marriage; it takes two to prosper. If a husband and wife will agree in prosperity and success - agreement means harmony - they will prosper. They'll have all the money they need to do what they want to do, when they want to do it. And when you have all the wealth you need to do what you want to do, when you want to do it, you're as rich as Croesus.

Both of them agreed to start a prayer process, night and morning, realizing that as they prayed for each other, there could not possibly be any bitterness, hostility or resentment, as divine love casts out everything unlike itself. And it does.

She prayed night and morning as follows: "My husband is God's man. God is guiding him to his true place. What he is seeking is seeking him. Divine love fills his soul. Divine peace fills his mind and heart. He is prospered in all his ways - spiritually, mentally, financially, socially - every way. By day and by night he's advancing, moving forward and growing spiritually, mentally, financially, socially, intellectually - in all ways, for life itself is growth. There are harmony, peace, love and understanding between us. It is divine right action and divine peace operating in our lives."

And he prayed for his wife night and morning as follows: "My wife is God's child. She's the daughter of the infinite, a child of eternity. Divine love fills her soul, and it is written, 'He careth for her'.

Divine love, peace, harmony and joy flow through her at all times. She is divinely guided and prospered in all her ways, for to prosper is to grow along all lines. There are harmony, peace, love and understanding between us. I salute the divinity in her and she salutes the divinity in me."

As both of them became relaxed and peaceful about the situation, they realized that only good can come out of this situation. Soon he received a phone call from the president of the company calling him back, stating that he had heard he had had a reconciliation with his wife. And at the same time, he praised him for his past achievements and accomplishments for the organization. Actually, his wife, without his knowledge, had visited the president of the company and had told the whole story; how happy they now were, and how the other woman had vanished out of his life. She told how they were now praying together. He was impressed, and she and her husband discovered very quickly the riches of scientific prayer, for the riches of the infinite are within you.

You can know if you have succeeded in prayer by the way you feel. If you remain worried or anxious, if you're wondering how, when, and where or through what source your answer will come, you are meddling. This indicates you do not really trust the wisdom of your subconscious. Avoid nagging yourself all day long or even from time to time. When you think of your desire, lightness of touch is important. Remind yourself that infinite intelligence is taking care of it in divine order far better than you can by tenseness of your conscious mind.

For example, if you say, "I need $5,000 by the fifteenth of next month", or "The judge must make a decision for me by the first of the month otherwise I'll lose my home, my mortgage", and so on, that's fear and anxiety and tension. What will that do? Bring blocks and delays and impediments into your life. Always go to the source. Remember: "In peace and in confidence shall be your strength". When you're anxious and tense and worried, that will not bring about prosperity or peace of mind, or health or anything. Go back to the source. Come to a place of absolute rest in your mind and say to yourself, and reiterate these truths: "It is done unto me as I believe. In all the ways as thousest believe, so be it done unto thee. All things be ready if the mind be so" - which means, all I have to do is ready in my mind to receive the benediction, the guidance, the wealth, the answer, the solution, the way out. "According to my faith is it done unto me. In all thy way thy faith hath made thee whole; go in peace, thy faith hath made thee whole. And all things are ready if the mind be so. The light of God shines in me. Peace of the everlasting God fills my soul. Quietness and confidence shall be my strength. God gave me richly all things to enjoy. With God all things are possible."

Reiterate these simple truths, and say: "The Lord is my Sheppard I shall not want; He maketh me to lie down in green pastures; He be with me beside the still waters; He restoreth my soul; When I call

upon him and he answers me; He'll be
with me in trouble; He'll set me on high
because he hath known my name. God is
my instant everlasting supply and ever-
present help in time of trouble".

Reiterate these truths. Read a Psalm like
the twenty-third and ninety-first Psalm.
And go over these Psalms quietly,
peacefully, and lovingly. You'll get to a
point of rest and peace in your mind, and
you'll realize that God is never late, and
that God is your instant and everlasting
supply, guiding and directing you,
revealing to you everything you need to
know, opening up the door for you,
revealing to you the solution. And God's
riches are circulating in your life and
there's always a surplus.

Then, when you act that attitude of mind, the way will open up. The dawn will appear and the shadows will clear away. But you won't get an answer by worrying, and fear and tension and anxiety. This will only attract more lack, more difficulties. So reverse it. Go back to the source. Reiterate the truths, you know. Dwell upon the truths of God, such as God is absolute peace, absolute harmony, boundless wisdom, infinite intelligence, the ever-living one, the all-wise one, the all-knowing one, the self-renewing one, knows all and sees all, the source of all blessings.

That will quiet your mind. That will give you peace. And the mind at peace always gets the answer, for "in quietness and in confidence shall be your strength". And God knows only the answer, so learn to let go and relax. Do not give power to the externals or conditions. Give power and allegiance to the infinite presence and power within you.

The swimming instructor tells you that you can float on the water which will support you if you remain quiet, still and at peace. But if you get nervous, tense, fearful, you will sink. When you are seeking wealth, prosperity, success, or a spiritual healing, or anything, feel that you are immersed in the holy presence. Feel like you're in the ocean or in a swimming pool, and realize the golden river of life, love, truth, and beauty are flowing through you now, transforming your whole being into the pattern of harmony, love peace and abundance. Feel yourself swimming in the great ocean of life. That sense of wellness will restore you; "For He restoreth my soul".

The following meditation will bring many wonderful things into your life. Listen to it and say, "These truths are sinking into my subconscious mind. I picture them going from my conscious to my subconscious like seeds I'm depositing in the soil. I know that I mold, fashion, and create my own destiny. My faith in the infinite being which created all things, and my faith in God is my fortune. This means an abiding faith in all things good. I live in the joyous expectancy of the best, and only the best comes to me. I know the harvest I will reap in the future because all my thoughts are God's thoughts and the power of God is with my thoughts of good. My thoughts are the seeds of goodness, truth, beauty, and abundance. I now place my thoughts of love, peace, joy, success, abundance, security and goodwill in the garden of my mind. This is God's garden. The glory and beauty of God will be expressed in my life and I will know if my garden will yield an abundant harvest. From this moment forward I express life, love and truth. I am radiantly happy and prosperous in all my ways, and God multiplies my good exceedingly."

To prosper means to succeed, to thrive, to turn out well. In other words, when you are prospering, you are expanding, growing spiritually, mentally, financially, socially and intellectually.

Never be envious or jealous of another person's wealth, or promotion, or their diamonds or jewels, for that would impoverish you; that would attract lack and limitation to you. Rejoice in their success, in their prosperity, in their wealth; and wish for them greater riches, because what you wish for the other you're wishing for yourself, for you are the only thinker. What you think about the other, you are creating in your own mind and body and experience, and also your pocketbook. This is why you rejoice in the success, in the prosperity, and in the millions that others have.

In order to truly prosper it is necessary that you become a channel through which the life principal flows freely, harmoniously, joyously and lovingly. I suggest that you establish a definite method of working and thinking, and that you practice it regularly and systematically every day.

One young man who consulted me had experienced a poverty complex for many years; had received no answers to his prayer. He had prayed for prosperity, but the fear of poverty continuously weighed on his mind, and naturally he attracted more lack and limitation than prosperity. The subconscious mind accepts the dominant of two ideas. Change your mind from belief in poverty, but begin to believe in God's riches which are all around you, infinite riches.

After talking with me he began to realize that his thought-image of wealth produces wealth; that every thought is created unless it is neutralized by a counter-thought of greater intensity.

Furthermore, he realized that his thought and belief about poverty was greater than his belief in the infinite riches all around him. Consequently, he changed his thoughts and kept them changed.

I wrote out a prosperity prayer for him as follows. It will benefit you: "I know there's only one source: the Life Principle, the Living Spirit from which all things flow. It created the universe and all things therein contained. I am a focal point of the divine presence. My mind is open and receptive. I am a free-flowing channel for harmony, beauty, guidance, wealth, and the riches of the infinite. I know that wealth, health, and success are released from within and appear in the without. I am now in harmony with the infinite riches within and without, and I know these thoughts are sinking into my subconscious mind and will be reflected on the screen of space. I wish for everyone all the blessings of life. I am open and receptive to the divine riches - spiritual, mental and material, and they flow to me in avalanches of abundance."

This young man focused his thoughts on God's riches, rather than on poverty, and made it a special point never to deny what he affirmed. Many people pray, you know, for wealth, and they deny it an hour later. They say, "I can't afford this; I can't make ends meet". They're making a mockery of their prayer. They're like the man who gets into a taxi in New York and he's going to the airport, and on the way he says to the taxi driver, "Oh, take me back home, I forgot my passport." So he goes back. Then he said on the way again, "Oh, I'd better go to my club, I forgot my wallet". So the taxi driver takes him to his club. And he says, "Oh, I forgot some letters at my grandmother's", so off he goes to the grandmother. And he gives a half a dozen directions in a half an hour to the taxi driver. Finally, the taxi driver takes him into the police station because he realizes he's mental.

Well, now this is the way millions of people pray, even in the new thought movement. They give a half a dozen directions to their subconscious mind in a half an hour or an hour. The subconscious is so confused and perplexed, it doesn't know what to do - it doesn't do anything! So it results in plain frustration. Frustration comes from the meaning to deceive; to work for nothing. So you don't put a seed in the ground and then dig it up. Stop contradicting what you affirmed! And that's the way people pray for prosperity. They're constantly denying what they're affirming, and they're making a mockery of prayer.

So this young man focused his thoughts on God's riches, rather than poverty, and he stopped saying, "I can't afford", or "I can't buy that piano", or "I can't buy that car". Never use the word "can't"; "can't" is the only devil in the universe. Your subconscious takes you literally and blocks all your good.

Now in a month's time his whole life was transformed. He affirmed the above truth, which I just mentioned, morning and evening, for about ten minutes, slowly and quietly, engraving them in his mind, knowing what he was doing, believing what he was doing.

Knowing that he was actually writing down these truths in his subconscious mind, causing the latter to be activated and to release its hidden treasures.

For the gold mine is in your subconscious. The diamond mine is there. It's the source of all the riches of heaven.

Although this man had been a salesman for ten years, there were rather dim prospects for the future. Suddenly he was made sales manager at $30,000 a year plus prime benefits. Your subconscious has ways that you know not of. It's impossible to impregnate your subconscious mind with the idea of wealth and be poor. It's impossible to impregnate your subconscious with the idea of success - and good heavens, you were born to win and succeed! The infinite can't fail! You were born to triumph.

Let your prayer be: "By day and by night I am advancing, moving forward and growing. God gave me richly all things to enjoy".

POINTERS TO REMEMBER

Serve yourself with the powers of your mind

1. Decide to be wealthy the easy way, with the infallible aid of your subconscious mind.

2. Trying to accumulate wealth by the sweat of your brow and hard labor is one way to become the richest man in the graveyard. You do not have to strive or slave hard.

3. Wealth is a subconscious conviction. Build into your mentality the idea of wealth.

4. The trouble with most people is that they have no invisible means of support.

5. Repeat the word, "Wealth," to yourself slowly and quietly for about five minutes prior to sleep and your subconscious will bring wealth to pass in your experience.

6. The feeling of wealth produces wealth. Keep this in mind at all times.
7. Your conscious and subconscious mind must agree. Your subconscious accepts what you really feel to be true. The dominant idea is always accepted

by your subconscious mind. The dominant idea should be wealth, not poverty.

8. You can overcome any mental conflict regarding wealth by affirming frequently, "By day and by night I am being prospered in all of my interests."

9. Increase your sales by repeating this statement over and over again, "My sales are improving every day; I am advancing, progressing, and getting wealthier every day."

10. Stop writing blank checks, such as, "There is not enough to go around," or "There is a shortage," etc. Such statements magnify and multiply your loss.

11. Deposit thoughts of prosperity, wealth, and success in your subconscious mind, and the latter will give you compound interest.

12. What you consciously affirm, you must not mentally deny a few moments later. This will neutralize the good you have affirmed.

13. Your true source of wealth consists of the ideas in your mind. You can have an idea worth millions of dollars. Your

subconscious will give you the idea you seek.

14. Envy and jealousy are stumbling blocks to the flow of wealth. Rejoice in the prosperity of others.

15. The block to wealth is in your own mind. Destroy that block now by getting on good mental terms with everyone.

Step up this way to riches

1. Be bold enough to claim that it is your right to be rich and your deeper mind will honor your claim.

2. You don't want just enough to go around. You want all the money you need to do all the things you want to do and when you want to do them. Get acquainted with the riches of your subconscious mind.

3. When money is circulating freely in your life, you are economically healthy. Look at money like the tide and you will always have plenty of it. The ebb and flow of the tide is constant. When the tide is out, you are absolutely sure that it will return.

4. Knowing the laws of your subconscious mind, you will always be supplied regardless of what form money takes.

5. One reason many people simply make ends meet and never have enough money is that they condemn money. What you condemn takes wings and flies away.

6. Do not make a god of money. It is only a symbol. Remember that the real riches are in your mind. You are here to lead a balanced life—this includes acquiring all the money you need.

7. Don't make money your sole aim. Claim wealth, happiness, peace, true expression, and love, and personally radiate love and good will to all. Then your subconscious mind will give you compound interest in all these fields of expression.

8. There is no virtue in poverty. It is a disease of the mind, and you should heal yourself of this mental conflict or malady at once.

9. You are not here to live in a hovel, to dress in rags, or to go hungry. You are here to lead the life more abundant.

10. Never use the terms "filthy lucre" or "I despise money." You lose what you criticize. There is nothing good or bad, but thinking of it in either light makes it so.

11. Repeat frequently, "I like money. I use it wisely, constructively, and judiciously. I release it with joy, and it returns a thousand fold."

12. Money is not evil any more so than copper, lead, tin, or iron which you may find in the ground. All evil is due to ignorance and misuse of the mind's powers.

13. To picture the end result in your mind causes your subconscious to respond and fulfill your mental picture.

14. Stop trying to get something for nothing. There is no such thing as a free lunch. You must give to receive. You must give mental attention to your goals, ideals, and enterprises, and your deeper mind will back you up. The key to wealth is application of the laws of the subconscious mind by impregnating it with the idea of wealth.

We have Book Recommendations for you

Joseph Murphy: Neutralizing Negative
Suggestions   (Audio MP3)

Joseph Murphy: The Unbelieveable Power
of Suggestion   (Audio MP3)

The Power of Your Subconscious Mind by
Joseph Murphy
ABRIDGED - (Audio CD)

The Power of Your Subconscious Mind by
Joseph Murphy
MP3 [UNABRIDGED] (Audio CD)
,HARDCOVER

Automatic Wealth: The Secrets of the
Millionaire Mind--Including: Acres of
Diamonds, As a Man Thinketh, I Dare you!,
The Science of Getting Rich, The Way to
Wealth, and Think and Grow Rich [

Think and Grow Rich [MP3 AUDIO]
[UNABRIDGED]
by Napoleon Hill, Jason McCoy (Narrator)
(Audio CD)

As a Man Thinketh [UNABRIDGED]
by James Allen, Jason McCoy (Narrator)
(Audio CD)

Your Invisible Power: How to Attain Your
Desires by Letting Your Subconscious
Mind Work for You [MP3 AUDIO]
[UNABRIDGED]
by Genevieve Behrend, Jason McCoy
(Narrator) (Audio CD)

Thought Vibration or the Law of Attraction
in the Thought World [MP3 AUDIO]
[UNABRIDGED]
by William Walker Atkinson, Jason McCoy
(Narrator) (Audio CD), Paperback

BN Publishing

Improving People's Life

www.bnpublishing.com

Lightning Source UK Ltd.
Milton Keynes UK
UKHW011823100619

344167UK00001B/245/P

9 789562 915243